A River Called Bearcamp

A River Called Bearcamp

Poems   Page P. Coulter

Photographs   Dale Lary

TOP OF THE WORLD PRESS · 2011

Acknowledgments

Ground Pine, She Ran with the Mountains, Rock: *Lakes Region Spirit*
I am Calm, Bearcamp River, Jack in the Pulpit: *Northern New England Review*

My thanks to Emilie for editing the poems.

Poems © 2011 Page P. Coulter
Photographs © 2011 Dale Lary
Top of the World Press
82 Top of the World Road, Sandwich NH 03227
WWW.PAGECOULTER.NET
ISBN 978-0-9815929-1-6

*To Amos and Etta,
whose searching eyes
have alerted me to
the magic of the river.*

Table of Contents

River Talk

River, I've Come Here to Talk	2
Four Katautas	4
Chocorua Swayed in the Sky	5
Weetamoo Fleeing	6
She Washed Her Hands in the River	8
Bearcamp River	11
Where I Swayed as a Child	12
Let's Begin by Walking	14
I've Lost My Heart	17

Conversations

Jack in the Pulpit	20
Love Broke	22
She Ran with the Mountains	23
Ground Pine	27
Rock	28
Conversations with Passaconaway	29
So Many Things	32
To Descartes, Walking Along the Bearcamp	33
What They Would Talk About	34

Talk to Me

Talk to Me	38
Viola Palustris	40
River Rondel	41
I Am Calm	42
Passaconaway's Dream	44
A Short History of a Child Growing Up	46
January Thaw	48
Sometimes I Climb to the Treehouse	49
Poem	51

River Talk

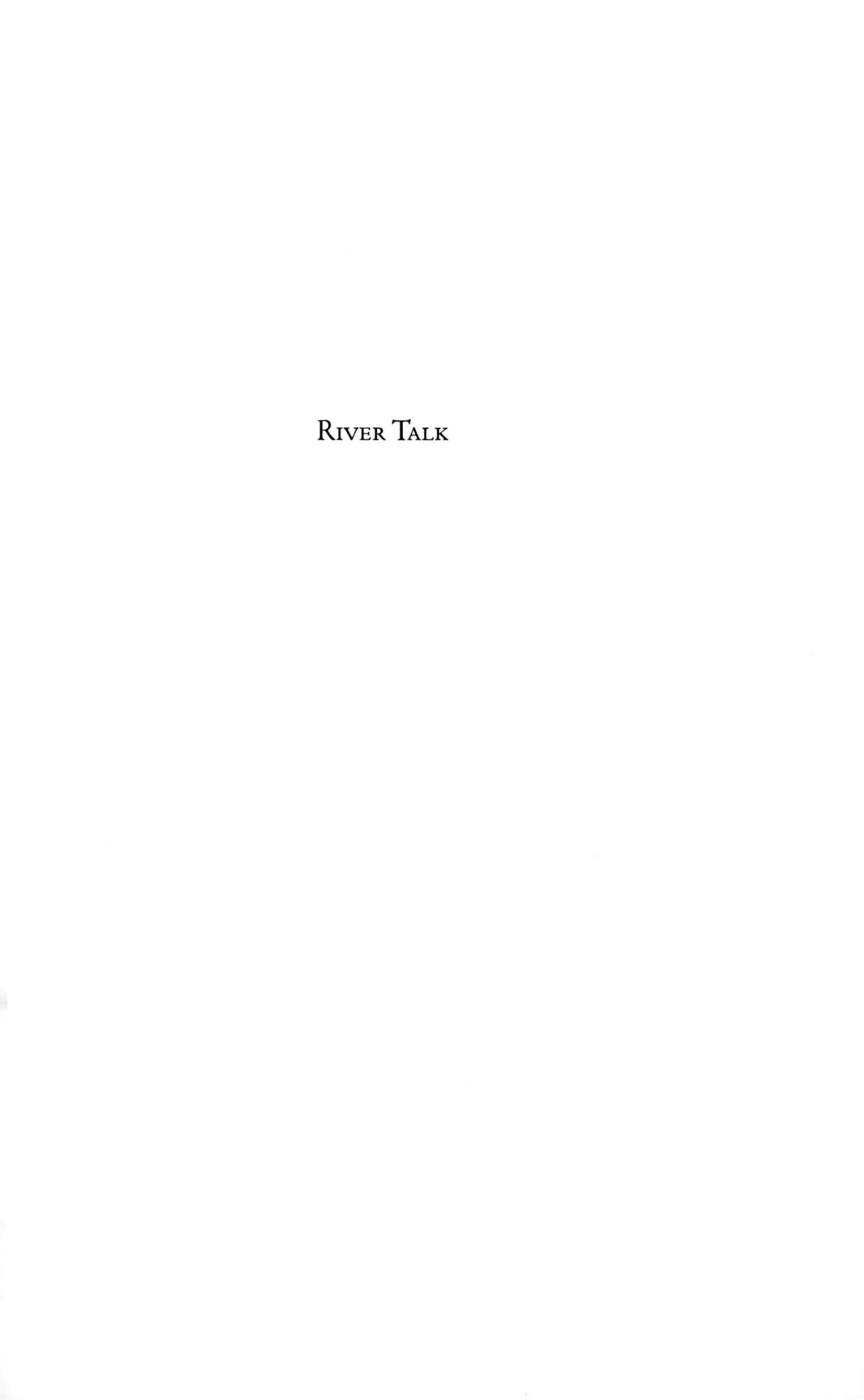

River, I've Come Here to Talk

River, I've come here to talk.
You, always in a rush to pass me
flinging yesterdays into the current of my will.

You, who think nothing of
dropping my sentiments
over the falls.

You, River, once read Anna Karenina to me,
while cooling my toes in your waters.
You held my secrets under your smooth stones.

You sang while the Civil War raged downstream.
You carried the blood of Metacom's people
as they fought for their land and pride.

Your pride is instinctive; it's who you are
as you flow, independent
of what happens beside you.

Why do the rest of us think tragedies
while you wind, like an unmanned
kayak, through centuries, oblivious?

Is it so we can come to your banks
to splash melodies of Bach and Mussorgsky
into our bland solicitude?

River, come stretch out beside me
and if I weep, let your sorrow
carry me across your stepping rocks.

Four Katautas

Why do rivers fly?
Dragons enkindle the wind
buoyant with froth, with sky.

Why do rivers sigh?
Let eddies swirl in backwash
all that could have been, now is.

Why do rivers cry?
Ecstasies of spring repent
nimbly, up-tempo, breakneck.

Why do rivers die?
Wet banks shouldering sorrow
dwindle in the sure current.

Chocorua Sways in the Sky

Chocorua sways
    as red night
        approaches
            candling its way

and the space
    between us wavers
        like a fancied flame
        or like a shell
            of sheltering light
                diminished
Nothing is
    the way it was
        a day ago
            Moments sway
                in our minds
                    and everything
                        moves on

Weetamoo Fleeing

Often she washed in the stream
rubbing alchemies into her hair culled from
fox-grape, roots of sassafras, and balsam.

And she would listen
to flute-like trills of wood thrush
fluttering in nearby shrubs

or to the raspy croaks of frogs
crouching, and water-logged
as they spoke about the universe.

No Black Berries hung from her ears,
her cells couldn't talk, and nothing but
stars and the moon ignited her sky.

Regrettably the magic
of wintergreen, sorrel, rattle box, and fern
would fade from our senses

when she drowned (in the self-same
riverbed) fleeing those who would
ravish our future.

She Washed Her Hands in the River

She washed her hands in the river
and the river cleansed them with nutrients gathered
as it ran across rocks and falls and swirling eddies.
She washed her hands in the river.

She washed her hands in the river
and the river spelled stories:
how Passaconaway squatted there on its banks,
teaching his son, Wonalancet, how to soak and bend his bow,
how to place notches in the shape of half moons
along its outer curve. They did it together
when the sun was only a sparkle of day.
She washed her hands in the river.

She washed her hands in the river
and the river taught her its language
full of r's, s's, and wayfaring w's.
Our language is lost, it sighed.
No one tries to learn it anymore.
Then wound away through a stand of hemlocks.
She washed her hands in the river.

She washed her hands in the river
and the river unraveled its history,
how it flowed down from nearby mountains
blessed by river nymphs, who let it play
through their long spindly fingers
as they tossed it over trillium, buttercups,
and trailing arbutus, how it wove through the
forest and fields where Chocorua and his son
and the settler's son romped and swam,
and whistled from trees,
how it etched a place in the earth
long before anyone was here to enjoy it.
She washed her hands in the river.

She washed her hands in the river
and the river bounced back its reflection
of her and the ghostly sky.
She gazed even down through its surface
and found not an image but a feeling,
a river of life and bones and death and stars
and gratitude. She was glad.
She washed her hands in the river.

Bearcamp River

He'd listened to *Paddle to the Sea* as a child,
watching in his mind the minuscule canoe
as it made its way downstream—
its rocky turns, spirit snakes,
its spits of reeds and sand, and
kingfishers cht-cht-cht-ing overhead.

A city boy by birth, now he walks along
the Bearcamp hearing its private messages
spelled out for him between its foam
and bubbly sputterings. Why shouldn't he
be mesmerized by its cryptic river codes,
winding his will around its sloppy inlets?

To what better way of life could he aspire than this,
here in this myriad of rivulets and dazzling planets
looming at every turn, away from famine, bombs,
and dwindling water supplies? Stream of his being,
stream of his consciousness, stream of his mind.

Hard of hearing now, he stoops to better catch
the cold stream's murmuring; a clump
of painted trillium nods from the bank.
Please put me back, the paddler calls,
    please put me back.

Where I Swayed as a Child

Where I swayed, fingers and toes, from pine tops
I sighted the wellspring of delight.

Where delight met my eyes from this spire of my world
I could feel the downbeat of power.

Where power rushed over my overalls and spine
sweet doves were nestling in the apricot of my heart.

Where my heart burst like a bat through the spiny branches
patience was signaling the stars.

Where the stars were groping through blue
I could feel impatience rummaging through my roots.

Where my roots rambled like a deaf man looking for his aid,
I shouted, *Grampa, send up a basket of chocolates.*

I tossed him a rope, tossed a pine cone through a cloud
where *where* is there up next to the sky, a prize.

Let's Begin by Walking

MONDAY

Patches and batches of *trillium* lapping at roadsides elegant as elephants flapping red-trillium ears three-lobed wake-robins or painted blazes in cups of brilliant white yawning and nodding

TUESDAY

Leafless corn lily's yellow bells of lemon lace-cupped *clintonia* on a lolly-stalk.

WEDNESDAY

Stout yellow-flowered *bellwort* shy and voluptuous delight in showering semantics or drafting drowsy dreamlets

THURSDAY
Dangling alabaster dalliance dangle from alternating leaves of *solomon's seal* wise Solomon of seven hundred wives and three hundred concubines all hanging-dangling compliantly in rows

FRIDAY
Algonquins padding paths in cleft-pink pouches of moccasin tanned leather footwear flowers wet through bogs though some would insist on sipping scents from *lady's slippers*

I've Lost My Heart

I walk down to the river bridge.
My heart leaps with joy.
Leaps out of my chest, dives into the current.

The dogs wag their tails and bark.
My heart bobs along.
Disappears under the bridge.

My heart has left me.
And where are my tears?
Yesterday I cried when you read from *Huckleberry Finn*.

The river is crimson with tenderness,
yet the trees stand like bones by the shore.
My love, I am gone as well.

Swallowed by the river.
When you lean down to kiss me,
my lips are cold.

I'm someone else, not me.
Where have I gone?
The river rushes merrily on.

Conversations

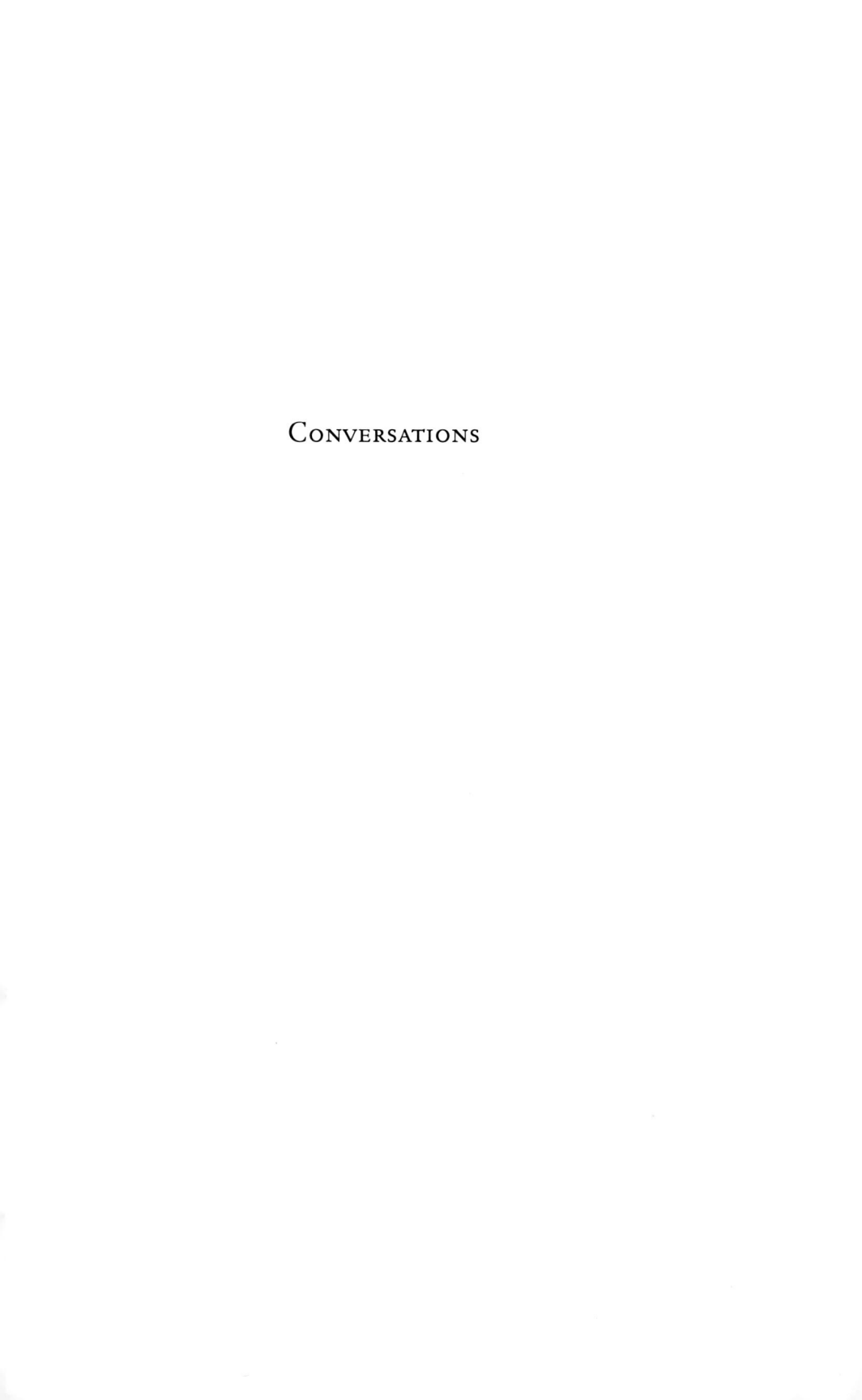

Jack in the Pulpit

Straight as a crochet hook
among green lapping tongues
of feathery ferns unfurling gossip
before the sermon begins.

From his upright stalk
he talks to slipper-like
lips of calypsos,
sorrel sprouts, and
star-eyed miterwort.

A long unending yarn
weaving over around and in
the fickle ferns' and flowers'
fantasies till they forget
where they are growing.

Love Broke

like a grave yard
of fallen stones
weeping grasses
and the slight scent
of trailing arbutus
under it all

She Ran with the Mountains

She ran with the mountains whenever they broke the sky.
She ran with the mountains and held them hostage
   because they were harbingers of un-foretold possessions.
She ran with the mountains and with her hands she spelled
   live free or die all over their rills.
She ran with the mountains.

She ran with the mountains in spring when they were wet
   with rivulets.
She ran with the mountains in summer when owls
   carried them with giant wingspans into the dark.
She ran with the mountains because they were there
   within reach and because she loved to run, too.

She ran with the mountains to places they'd never seen before.
   They sped past Nepal, Mont Blanc, and the Picos of Spain.
   They never stopped. They ran in circles around the poles.
She ran with the mountains, she ran with the mountains,
   she ran and ran. They ran.
She ran with the mountains on Thursdays
   beyond the beyond where nets of clouds would catch them.
She ran with the mountains.

She ran with the mountains to find out who she wasn't or was.
    They cut holes in the sky on a dare. They romped.
She ran with the mountains with the future and past
    as if they knew each other's minds.
She ran with the mountains in autumn when fables dried up
    flowing deep into hidden springs.
She ran with the mountains.

She ran with the mountains to other worlds where silence
  was all there was.
She ran with the mountains because peace is what she was after.
  Peace and lemon ferns and vernal pools full of tadpoles.
She ran with the mountains where the sad dust of a moose print
  reminded her that everything was helpless and unaccounted for.
She ran with the mountains.

Ground Pine

Umbrella-like, we
make our own traces
held fast by our roots.

No one calls out *where,*
go this way, come here.
No one asks, *how soon?*

We are free to be
who we are. We like
our travelling style.

Simply root, stem, leaves
mint green, we flourish
now in November.

We carry dew-frost
silently near paths
dense with deer prints

songs of coyote,
musky scents of moose.
We are everywhere

unnoticed; we calm
the timbered forest
with our quiet charm.

If your feet be firm
ye are the angels.*

*Bahá'í Faith

Rock

sleepy hulk
stern as
an elephant's flank

bedded by the roadside
devouring last sun
wrapt
in copper-ochre

fallings
an eye-width of
beastly pleasure

Conversations with Passaconaway

1.
Not much, he says
when asked what he'd left behind.
Not much at all.
But I look for signs of you
wherever you might have been.
*Notice rocks and ferns and the magnificent pine,
Listen for the whirr of a chickadee's wings,
Watch how the sun strays stealthily across the mountains.*

2.
And something else.
What's that, Passaconaway?
*I like your dogs. I hunt with them at night.
The white-faced one I call her Fetch.
The one with no wagger, I call her Streak.*

And you, he says, *you come too—we laugh
and look for feathers and partridge eggs,
and hives of honey bees.*

3.
Passaconaway, I ask one day, as we
warm our toes in front of his mountain cave,
Why not come visit me some day?
Why would I want to do that?
Isn't there anything you'd like to revisit?
Not really, he says. *No,* he says, *not really.
Well maybe there is, now that I think of it:
Red Hill Pond, you call it, the one with the bog,
and the delicate orchids at the far end. I'd come
if only for that.* The sun makes him squint,
and a chickadee hops to his shoulder.

4.
We'll pull up that dug-out canoe, he says,
from the shallows in front of the bog.
Passaconaway, oh Passaconaway, I say
leaning into his over-sized heart.

5.
Passaconaway, why did you?
Why did I what?
Why did you wander off to Maine
where no one could find you?
He draws in a breath and sighs
the way our old dog Simon sighs
when all the doors in the house are shut.
As if all the fire of his life
were extinguished with that one breath.

6.
Club mosses cushion our feet as he guides me
down the path to his favorite pond,
and trees wave their limbs as we pass.
There in the silence of the Ossipees,
Peace, he whispers, *Peace to the beavers
and chittering birds and the goggle-eyed moose,
ankle deep in a pool, Peace to the quivering bog,
as still as November, Peace,* he calls,
as we paddle across to the orchids.

7.
Tell me, Passaconaway, how you make a burst
of fire in the middle of a pond? I ask.
Secrets are the breath of man, he says,
and he breathes breath into the pond and me.
A burst of flame. He's gone.

So Many Things

All the trees are leafing out,
  though last night's frost
    must have surprised them.

A wren flies nervously from its nest
  under porch beams to the wheel barrow
    balanced against the wood pile.

A crow pecks its underwing.
  Chill winds investigate the leaves.
    A stack of logs lies ready to be milled

It's just that the wind is
  always discovering things.
    How like death that must feel.

If I knew the names of butterflies,
  I'd name the one that landed on an aster,
    but these days names escape me.

To Descartes, Walking Along the Bearcamp

Curling through trees
a concert of water
plays the afternoon light—
and blocks of snow-covered ice
stacked against strewn rocks
let fantasies rush by
in bubbly disregard.

No race with time
no bleak desire
no jealousies
interfere with its flow.
No motion is stopped
nor pocketed to run another day.

It's like a wristwatch
self-winding, self-possessed—
mainspring
of converging currents,
rivulets, and bottom fish.

What path shall I follow in life?

What They Would Talk About

I took Descartes with me
down the Bearcamp Trail
one day last spring.

I thought we'd find
Passaconaway
at Charlie's Bridge

and they'd talk about magic
or nature's origins
by the roar of the waterfall.

All I wanted
was to see them together
in the waning light of their century

laughing and sharing anecdotes
in the loose world
of their visions.

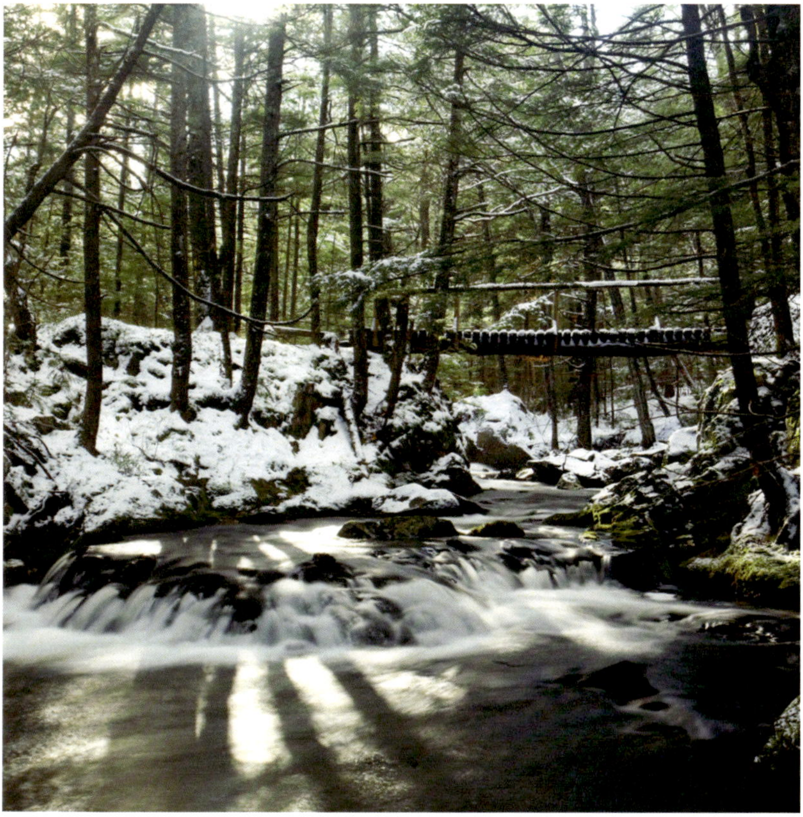

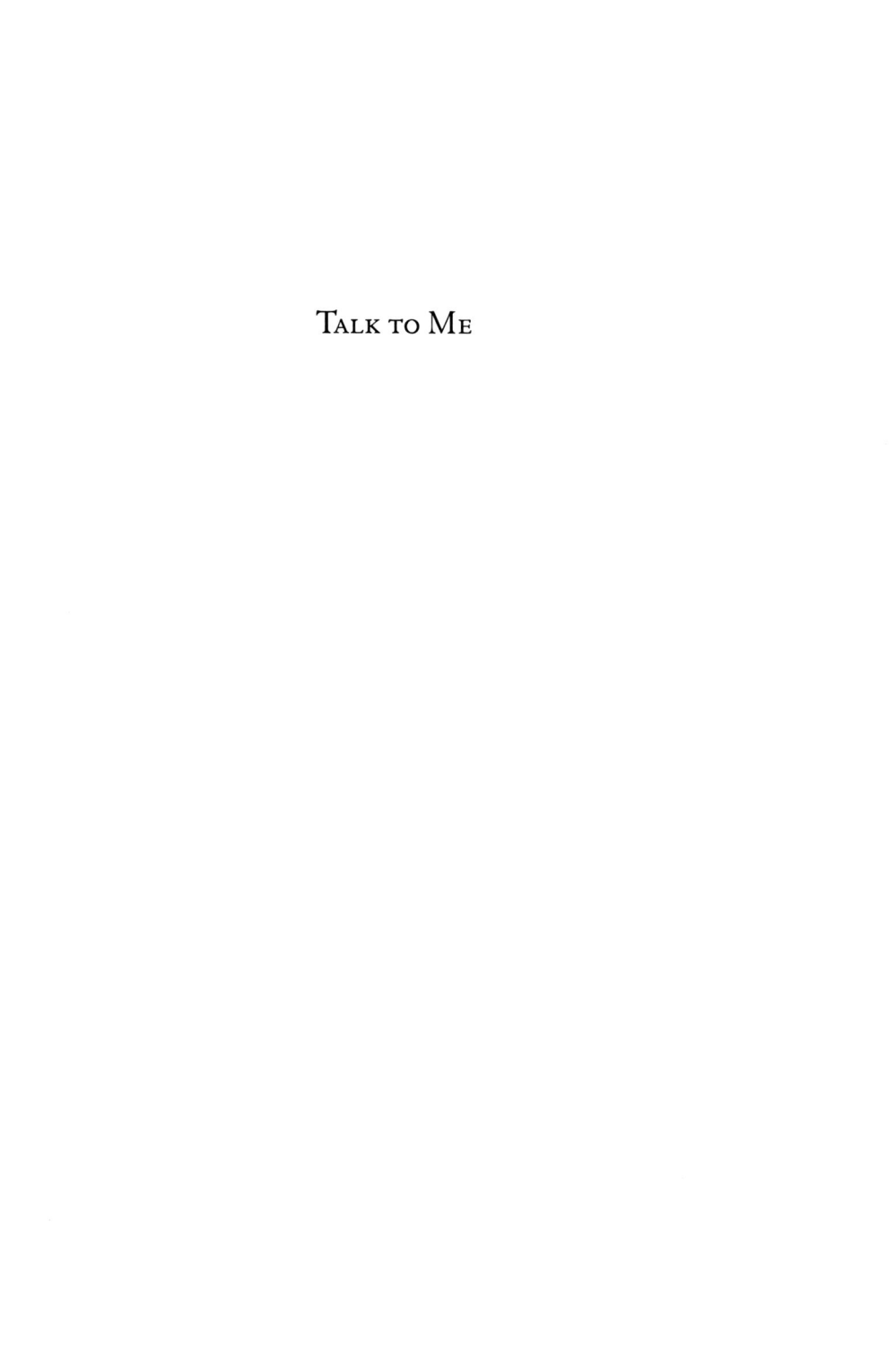

Talk to Me

Talk to Me

As I cross the bridge,
the river reaches up,
grabs me around the neck.
Talk to me, it murmurs.
Sometimes a river gets lonely.

It burbles and babbles,
hard for old ears to understand.

Passaconaway often sits on my banks, it purls.
To show me his fire tricks.
I hold his flame for hours: flames of trust, of setting
suns, of appetite.
Into my currents, eddies and side streams.

Here, the river loses itself in memories,
taking me through stick piles, river rat holes,
and overhanging logs.
Years pass. The river runs.
I see Passaconaway watching from the bank.

At last the river lets go of me.
Passaconaway is gone.
I toss a ringed stone over the bridge.
For luck and nourishment.
My hair is white as soda ash.
I too am gone.

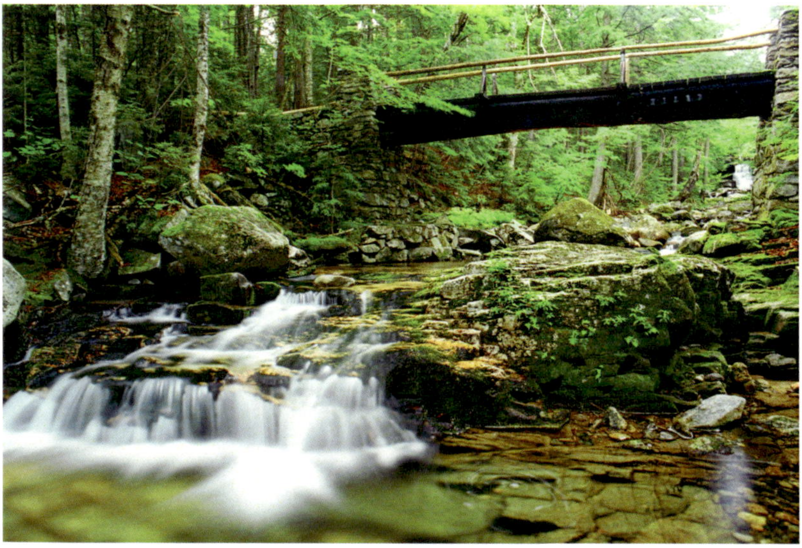

Viola Palustris

Clinging to a granite shelf
heart-leafed alpine violet
tell me, whose wise handiwork
holds you to this certainty?

River Rondel

Where rivers wind their way
    through forests ripe and bold,
too few will doze today,
    their fingers tinged with cold.

I fear the lost foothold
    on nature's interplay
where rivers wind their way
    through forests ripe and bold.

Their murmuring soft soufflé
    is distanced multifold
from cities' brass decay
    wherein one can't behold
where rivers wind their way
    through forests ripe and bold.

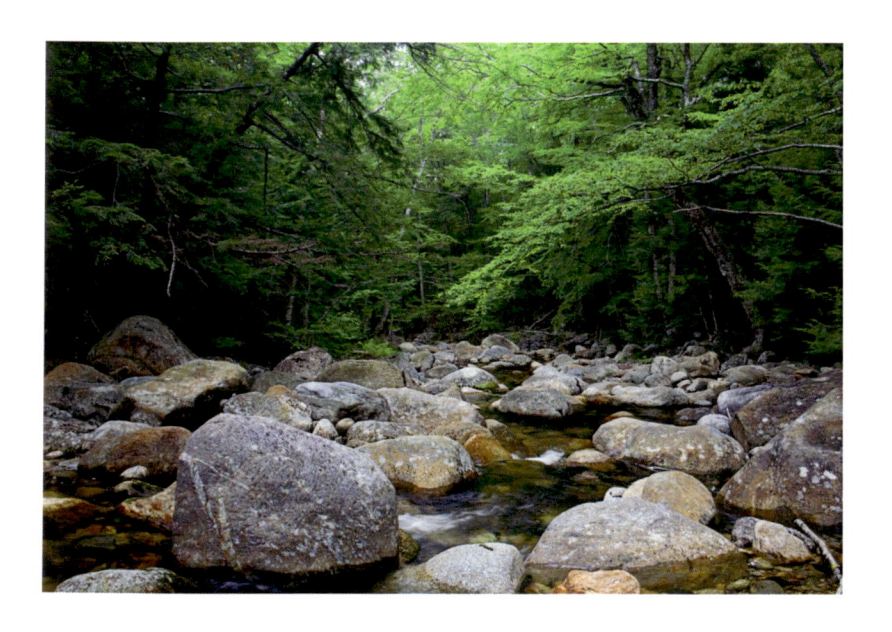

I Am Calm

I like to hear my snowshoes play
   sonatas in the snow. The poles
      release a slow continuo while

mouse trails cross the melody
   like notes in search of
      a sheltered glen to sing.

Cloven tracks of a moose
   compose a sarabande making
      me stop to listen. I am calm.

A sudden stream—a gigue
   intensifies—a bird swoops out of
      a hemlock, blue as a tune.

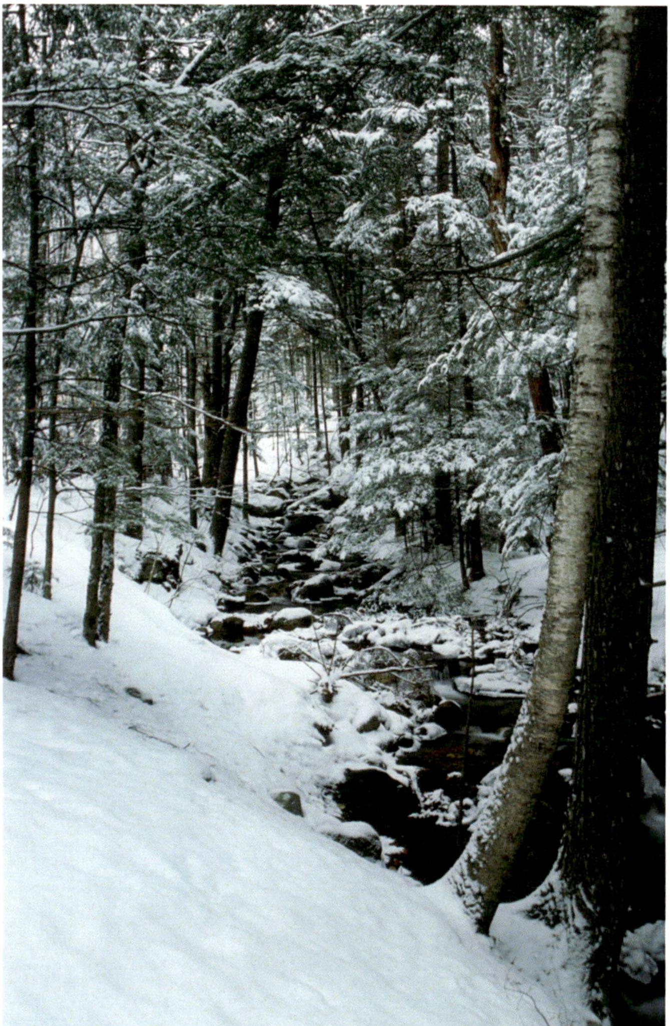

Passaconaway's Dream

Passaconaway and I are entering each other's dreams. His dream:
he's wearing a wolf-head mask, and he's scratching for water
at a frozen river's edge. My dream: I'm wearing oversize shoes
that keep me afloat across rocky frozen clouds. He says,
   This is so hard because I'm dead and you're not.
Don't worry, I say. Here, take this dream: I'm flying a small plane
between leaning trees. Under the trees, people wave flags I can't decipher.
   Peace, Passaconaway says, landing the plane in the
middle of a pond. We sit on the beach eating fresh goat cheese and dried
corn he takes from a packet on his belt.
   Not so hard after all, he smiles,
and how we feast, Passaconaway and I. We hardly notice the wolves
gathering around us to sing.

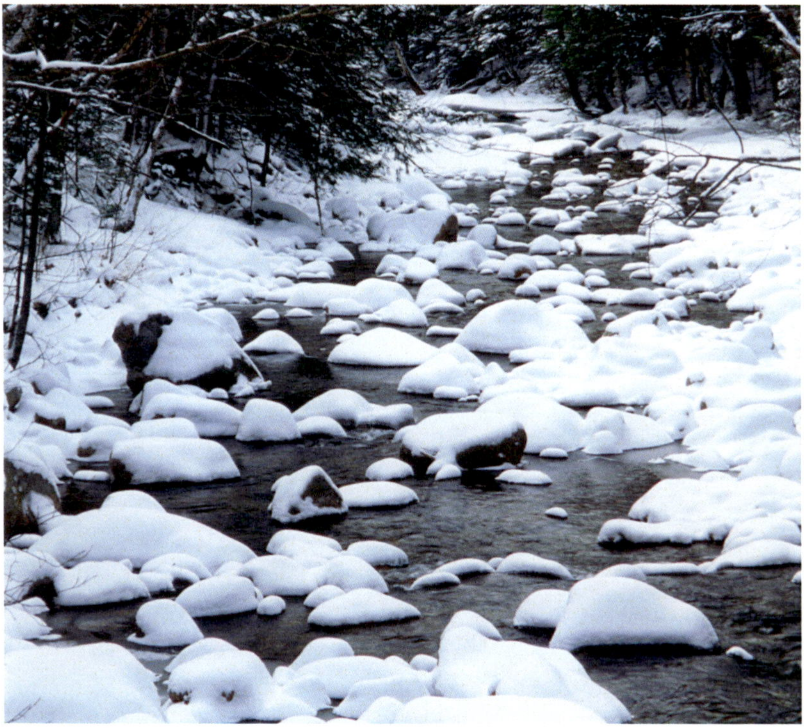

A Short History of a Child Growing Up

I grew up
laughing with the pines.
They held me prisoner.

They brushed against my window
calling me outside
and I went because they smelled
like scented candles
and the whistling out-of-doors.

They swayed from great heights
and when I scaled them
sap stuck to my fingers and knees.
I didn't care.
I entered their prison willingly.

I quarried gum from their trunks,
bathed in their freedom, high
and away from my mother's tears.

They told how wind
will suddenly change direction
flinging birds or thunder
through the skies, or how,
in winter, trees pull into themselves
to meditate snow and frost away.

I touched their bark, explored it
with my fingers even as my brother Jack
lay trying to breathe
through an iron lung.

They watched me skate on the turtle pond
or row the Locomosalou, lazily
through summer lily pads.

They said, "Knit wind wherever needles graze."
They said, "Turn back ribbed dawn
where spiders weep and pray."
They said," Go quickly into dark
where beavers weave syllables
into light."

They lent me needles to sew up
loss and distance and growth.

And when my mother called me back
to wash my face, grow up, be a debutante,
turtles giggled, spiders spun conundrums,
beavers guffawed in their lavish lodges,
and the pines, my pines, trilled
longing intermezzos.

January Thaw

Winter woods are like perfection of calm:
The snow flows down, but stops at the rim of a stream.

The woods are still, and my snowshoes whisper a Psalm
through the trees. It's the start of the January thaw;

the dead are preparing hammocks for the young.
The waters are still and the woods are calm.

Somewhere pastures thrive with no other meaning but green.

Sometimes I Climb to the Tree House

Sometimes I climb to the tree house in the old bull pine
beyond our field where time abandons meaning,
where the sun settles down between the trees

and the moon shows up like a kumquat.
It's my place: an earthly cluster of ideas,
all mine, an ideal arrangement for me alone.

Let's say the sun, as it swims to its own definition of time,
clamps its rays on Chocorua, or the moon laughs as it
jumps out from Maine's dense hills, or snowy branches sing

in total dissonance to the thrumming of a following stream.
Would that be bewildering? Would it cause me to tumble
down from my thoughts, to dinner fare or time's other needs?

Sometimes I dream in the old bull pine behind my house,
a bubble wherein my thoughts are gathered as breath,
blown up over the mountains like undomesticated ghosts.

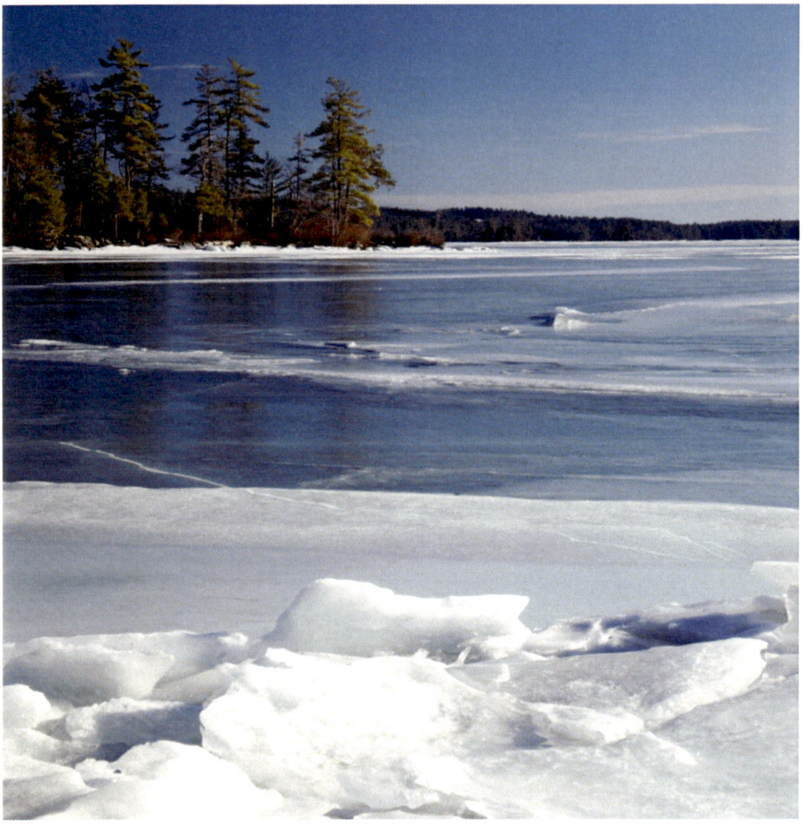

Poem

River, sing softly through the trees.
Carry the whisper song of siskens
and ravens' chalky *crruk*
as they check their reflection
in the flattened calm of your flow.

Add harmony to the gentle lift of hemlocks
leaning over you, and to the cold rocks
pounding bass notes under your melody.

Turn where no one expects it.
Change will lighten your current course
through fields of redbirds nesting
in almost forgotten farmlands.
River, stay calm.
Let your waters brim over the earth.

A River Called Bearcamp
was designed by Bruce Kennett,
who set the text in W. A. Dwiggins'
Winchester types. Printed and bound by
Penmor Lithographers on acid-free
Cougar Text and Cover.